ULTIMATE
NHL
Road Trip

By Will Graves

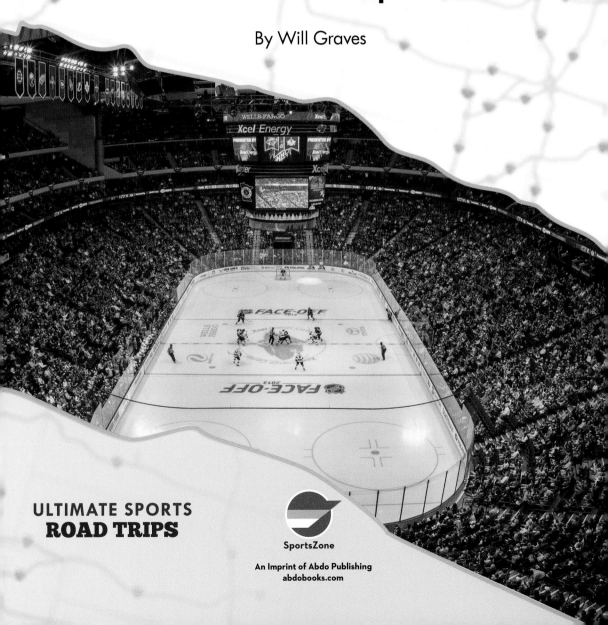

ULTIMATE SPORTS
ROAD TRIPS

SportsZone

An Imprint of Abdo Publishing
abdobooks.com

ABDOBOOKS.COM

Printed in the United States of America, North Mankato, Minnesota
092018
012019

THIS BOOK CONTAINS
RECYCLED MATERIALS

Cover Photo: Brad Rempel/Icon Sportswire
Interior Photos: Brad Rempel/Icon Sportswire, 1; Minas Panagiotakis/Getty Images Sport/Getty Images,
4–5; Marcio Jose Bastos Silva/Shutterstock Images, 7; Elise Amendola/AP Images, 8; Yoon S. Byun/Boston
Globe/Getty Images, 11; iStockphoto, 13, 31, 44; Ron Frehm/AP Images, 14; David Hahn/Icon Sportswire/
AP Images, 16; Jeanine Leech/Icon Sportswire/Getty Images, 19; Jeanine Leech/Icon Sportswire/AP
Images, 20; Richard Cavalleri/Shutterstock Images, 23; Richard Wolowicz/Getty Images Sport/Getty
Images, 24, 45; Torontonian/Alamy, 27; JHVE Photo/Shutterstock Images, 28; Dave Reginek/National
Hockey League/NHLI/Getty Images, 32; Hannah Foslien/Getty Images Sport/Getty Images, 35; Andy
King/AP Images, 37; Nick Wosika/Icon Sportswire/AP Images, 38; Pressefoto Ulmer/Ullstein Bild/Getty
Images, 41; Tony Gutierrez/AP Images, 42

Editor: Bradley Cole
Series Designer: Melissa Martin

Library of Congress Control Number: 2018949188

Publisher's Cataloging-in-Publication Data

Names: Graves, Will, author.
Title: Ultimate NHL road trip / by Will Graves.
Description: Minneapolis, Minnesota : Abdo Publishing, 2019 | Series: Ultimate sports road trips |
        Includes online resources and index.
Identifiers: ISBN 9781532117565 (lib. bdg.) | ISBN 9781532170423 (ebook)
Subjects: LCSH: Sports arenas--Juvenile literature. | Sports spectators--Juvenile literature. | Hockey--
        Juvenile literature. | National Hockey League--Juvenile literature.
Classification: DDC 796.962097--dc23

TABLE OF CONTENTS

Drop the
PUCK!

The first hockey rinks weren't rinks at all. People skated on frozen ponds in Canada. The new sport gave the game's first players something to do during the long, cold winters.

The weather in Canada isn't always great. So eventually the game began to make its way indoors. The first organized indoor hockey game was played on March 3, 1875, at Victoria Skating Rink in Montreal.

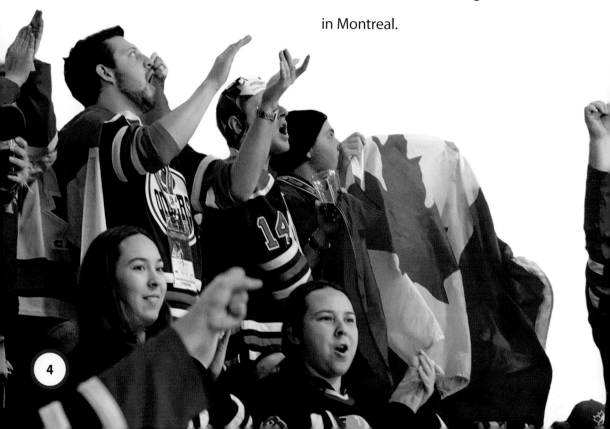

There were no comfy seats, big buckets of popcorn, video replays, or goal horns. Times have changed. Going to a game these days is an entirely different experience. Laser shows light up the ice before games. Other entertainment includes trivia contests and special songs when the home team scores. And sometimes in Detroit, octopuses fly through the air.

Nearly 150 years after that first organized indoor game in Montreal, National Hockey League (NHL) arenas are packed from Florida to British Columbia. From California to Massachusetts, fans are waving their rally towels and launching into chants.

This road trip will showcase the ultimate NHL arenas. Although the venues in many of these places are new, they are almost all in cities with a long and decorated hockey history. Many of the arenas are in parts of town that have a lot to explore beyond the game.

Fans at NHL games take in great game experiences with chants, lights, and plenty of team spirit.

TD GARDEN

T he original Boston Garden saw a lot of history during its long run as the home of the Boston Bruins. The Bruins are one of the NHL's original six teams, and they played at the old Garden from 1928 through 1995. They won five Stanley Cups there behind stars such as Bobby Orr and Phil Esposito. A total of 57 Bruins players have been inducted into the Hockey Hall of Fame. Many of them played in the old Boston Garden.

The Garden wasn't always a fun place to catch a game. There was no air conditioning, and when it got too hot during the playoffs in the spring, a layer of fog would sometimes cover the ice. The NHL had to cancel a game in the 1988 Stanley Cup Final between the Bruins and the Edmonton Oilers because the power went out.

There are no such problems at the new TD Garden. First, the air conditioning keeps players and fans from overheating during

TD GARDEN

Boston, Massachusetts

Date Opened: September 30, 1995
Capacity: 17,565
Home Team: Boston Bruins

the spring. More seating has been added, and the seats are even wider now.

The food options at TD Garden feature a lot of local flavor, including seafood. Fans can eat lobster rolls—a New England delicacy—or maybe a bowl of New England clam chowder. If junk food hits the spot, TD Garden has a "test kitchen" that lets patrons mix and match favorite snack options. Visitors can choose from Cheetos Popcorn or a walking taco topped with Doritos to give it an extra crunch. There are even Cheetos waffles and chicken sandwiches to fill up on in case the game goes into overtime.

FUN FACT

TD Garden also hosts the annual Beanpot Tournament between four Boston-area college hockey teams: Boston University, Boston College, Northeastern University, and Harvard University.

Fans should make sure to find their seats early. The pregame party is not to be missed. Right before faceoff the crowd passes around a giant flag with the Bruins' logo on it. Then the puck drops, and the game begins. Visitors should also take a few minutes to count all the banners hanging from the rafters.

Nathan Horton (right) celebrates his goal against the Tampa Bay Lightning in the 2011 playoffs.

Between the Bruins and their National Basketball Association (NBA) buddies the Boston Celtics, Boston has celebrated a lot of championships.

If fans need to stretch their legs between periods, they can head up to Levels 5 and 6. There they can check out The Sports Museum. The museum is broken up into sections by sport and allows visitors to learn about everything from hockey to football to the Boston Marathon. The museum has an amazing half-mile (0.8 km) of exhibits about the history of Boston sports inside TD Garden. Local elementary and middle school students visit the museum every year as part of an educational program.

The Bruins created lasting memories during Game 7 of the 2011 Eastern Conference finals. With just 7:33 left in regulation, Boston's Nathan Horton scored the only goal in a 1–0 home victory over the Tampa Bay Lightning. That sent the Bruins to the Stanley Cup Final. The Vancouver Canucks

FUN FACT

Nathan Horton took a little bit of TD Garden with him to the 2011 Stanley Cup Final. He poured water from the Garden onto the ice at Rogers Arena in Vancouver before Game 7 to make it feel a little more like home. The Bruins won 4–0 and raised a sixth Cup banner to the rafters at TD Garden the following fall.

took Boston to another Game 7 in Vancouver, but Boston brought home its sixth Stanley Cup.

Bruins fans have watched their team bring home six Stanley Cups, including one at TD Garden in 2011.

MADISON
SQUARE
GARDEN

Madison Square Garden (MSG) is one of the most famous arenas in the country. It hosts hockey, basketball, and some of the biggest concerts. There have actually been four Madison Square Gardens through the years, with each one bigger and better than the last.

When the original MSG opened in 1879, it didn't have a roof, so owner William Kissam Vanderbilt decided to call it a "Garden." The name stuck, though, as the venue hopscotched across the borough of Manhattan in New York City. MSG eventually gained a roof.

The current version of the Garden is found at the corner of 31st Street and 8th Avenue in New York City. It opened for hockey in 1968, making it the oldest active venue in the league by a wide margin. But MSG received a face-lift in 2013 that makes it one of

MADISON SQUARE GARDEN

New York City, New York

Date Opened: February 11, 1968
Capacity: 18,006
Home Team: New York Rangers

the most modern arenas in the world.

MSG is a busy place. It serves as the home of the New York Rangers and basketball's New York Knicks. It also hosts everything from concerts and boxing matches to college basketball tournaments and the Westminster Kennel Club Dog Show.

Going to a hockey game at the Garden provides a unique experience for fans' eyes and ears. During a stoppage in play fans can likely hear organist Ray Castoldi playing familiar tunes. He has been playing in a tiny booth near the top of the arena since 1989. Castoldi pumps out "Let's Go Rangers" and also wrote a song called "Slapshot" that plays every time the Rangers score a goal. Castoldi plays a big part in the Rangers' traditions at MSG. The organ gives the arena an old-school feel, but there are plenty of high-tech amenities at the game.

Mark Messier's goal against the Vancouver Canucks in the 1994 Stanley Cup Final is one of MSG's most memorable moments.

Fans should stop by RangersTown before the game or between periods. While there, fans can test their shooting accuracy and speed by firing pucks at a virtual Rangers goaltender. Fans can also write a word of encouragement to the Blueshirts, as the Rangers are known, on the community board. And a replica dressing stall allows fans to throw on a helmet and grab some gloves to see

 Chris Kreider (20) is one of the the leaders of the Rangers teams that now play at Madison Square Garden.

what they would look like as part of the team.

Rangers fans are a big part of the experience at the Garden. On June 14, 1994, the Rangers ended a 54-year drought between Stanley Cups when they beat the Vancouver Canucks in Game 7 of the Cup Final. One fan wrote on a sign, "Now I can die in peace!" But even during the drought, Rangers fans still filled the Garden, making it one of the best places in the world to catch a hockey game.

FUN FACT

The Rangers have a circular locker room thanks to former team captain Mark Messier. He thought if the locker room was a circle instead of a square, it would help bring the team together. The Rangers won the Stanley Cup the next season.

3 PPG PAINTS
ARENA

The house that Mario Lemieux built—with a major assist from Sidney Crosby—almost didn't happen. The Pittsburgh Penguins were in serious trouble even after drafting "Sid the Kid" in 2005. Though Crosby's arrival brought new life to the franchise, the Penguins still played in "The Igloo," which was aging badly. There was talk the team would relocate from Pittsburgh to Kansas City.

In March 2007 the team reached an agreement to build PPG Paints Arena. By the time it opened in 2010 across the street from where the Igloo once stood, Crosby had led Pittsburgh to a Stanley Cup and the Penguins were among the most popular teams.

The plan to build a new arena came together thanks to Lemieux, one of the game's all-time greats. He led Pittsburgh to Stanley Cups in 1991 and 1992. Then he bought the Penguins in 1999 and spent years helping land a deal that made sure the team stuck around. The result is a gleaming hockey palace in the heart

PPG PAINTS ARENA

Pittsburgh, Pennsylvania

Date Opened: August 18, 2010
Capacity: 18,387
Home Team: Pittsburgh Penguins

of Pittsburgh. It also happens to have a 10-foot (3-m) statue of Lemieux out front. The statue commemorates a spectacular goal by Lemieux against the New York Islanders in 1988.

 Sidney Crosby is among the NHL's biggest modern stars.

Once inside, the Wall of Champions is a good place to start a tour. It highlights past Penguins greats. Next, visitors should check out the sea of jerseys from various minor leagues and youth hockey teams along a wall in the concourse.

Crosby is one of the best reasons to catch a game at PPG Paints Arena. The superstar goes through the same routine before every game. He always practices his stickhandling on the golden M of the McDonald's logo near center ice.

The team's long run of success has turned the Penguins into one of the toughest tickets in the NHL. The Penguins sold out their February 14, 2007, game against Chicago, starting a streak of sellouts that topped more than 500 consecutive games by the end of the 2017–18 season. The team has done its best to give fans their money's worth. During the sellout streak the Penguins have won three Stanley Cups.

FUN FACT

Fans who step into the concourse to grab a Primanti Brothers sandwich, a Pittsburgh specialty that comes with French fries on top, won't miss a minute of the action. The arena features more than 800 HD televisions so spectators can keep up even if they're not in their seats.

BELL CENTRE

Montreal might just be the hockey capital of the world. The city in the Canadian province of Quebec has a long and storied relationship with the sport. The first indoor hockey game was in Montreal.

The Bell Centre is the latest home for the NHL's Montreal Canadiens, the most successful franchise in league history. The Canadiens have won 24 Stanley Cups, far more than any other team in the league. During each of those seasons, they played at the historic Montreal Forum.

The Forum served as the site of some of the NHL's greatest teams. The Canadiens won five straight Cups in the 1950s under coach Toe Blake and won four in the 1970s under coach Scotty Bowman.

Unlike in places such as Pittsburgh, where the old arena was torn down to help pave the way for the new arena, the Forum is still standing. It's considered an official Canadian historic site.

BELL CENTRE

Montreal, Quebec, Canada

Date Opened: March 16, 1996
Capacity: 21,287
Home Team: Montreal Canadiens

 Canadiens fans pack the Bell Centre to support their team.

It's definitely worth a quick trip to visit the site where Montreal's legends dominated the NHL.

The Canadiens have moved slightly more than a mile (2 km) away to the Bell Centre, which holds more than 21,000 fans. It's one of the largest venues in the NHL. And the place is packed every winter with fans there to cheer on the *bleu, blanc, et rouge* (blue, white, and red).

Taking a tour of the Bell Centre on non-game days provides a taste of the team's history. Fans can visit the dressing room, where some of the Canadiens' Hall of Famers—more than 50 and counting—are honored. There are also plaques highlighting every pro hockey season in Montreal since the team was formed in 1910.

> **FUN FACT**
>
> "To you from failing hands we throw the torch. Be yours to hold it high." These words appear both on the locker room wall and inside the Canadiens game sweaters. They are from Canadian poet John McCrae's "In Flanders Fields."

Upstairs in the Alumni Lounge, fans might encounter one of the past Montreal greats. They can even pose for a picture at the podium where the Canadiens coach speaks before and after games.

To get a real sense of Montreal's dominance, a trophy case includes a replica of each of the two dozen Stanley Cups the franchise has won. No other NHL club has won more than 13.

5 SCOTIABANK
ARENA

Team Canada played the 2016 World Cup of Hockey in Scotiabank Arena, then called Air Canada Centre, in Toronto, Ontario. The tournament came down to the last three minutes of the final. Canada was losing 1–0. Then Patrice Bergeron tied the game. Canada's Brad Marchand scored the eventual winning goal in the final minute of the third period. Led by captain Sidney Crosby, Canada earned a 2–1 win over Team Europe to capture the gold medal.

When the road trip gets to Toronto, there is an important stop before the Scotiabank Arena. The day begins approximately 2 miles (3.2 km) away at the birthplace of the modern NHL, Maple Leaf Gardens.

The arena built by former Toronto Maple Leafs owner and Hockey Hall of Famer Conn Smythe was known as "Canada's Cathedral of Hockey." It served as the home of the Maple Leafs from 1931 until 1999. The Leafs won 11 Stanley Cups during their

SCOTIABANK ARENA

Toronto, Ontario, Canada

Date Opened: February 9, 1999
Capacity: 18,800
Home Team: Toronto Maple Leafs

 Legends Row outside of Scotiabank Arena pays tribute to former Toronto Maple Leafs stars.

time at Maple Leaf Gardens. The arena also hosted the NHL's first All-Star Game in 1947.

After stopping by the Gardens, make sure to carve out some time for the Hockey Hall of Fame on Yonge Street just a short walk from Scotiabank Arena.

The Hall of Fame takes a deep dive into the history of the game. Visitors can learn about the hundreds of Hall of Fame members and browse the largest collection of hockey memorabilia in the world. Fans can watch a 3-D movie in one of the two movie theaters and even get their photos taken with the actual Stanley Cup. The Stanley Cup has been all over the world. But through 2017–18, the Leafs haven't won it since 1967.

After indulging in hockey super-fandom, it's time to finally get to the game. Since the Leafs moved to Air Canada Centre, as the arena was known in 1999, the arena has been a go-to sports destination. The arena hosted the 2000 NHL All-Star Game, the 2016 World Cup of Hockey, the 2016 NBA All-Star Game, and the 2015 International Ice Hockey Federation Under-20 World Championships.

FUN FACT

It takes anywhere from four to six hours for the arena to be converted from a basketball arena to a hockey arena.

The main draw besides the Maple Leafs is the food. Fans should come to Scotiabank Arena hungry. Concession stands have great options for a sweet tooth, including deep-fried Twix and funnel cake fries.

A wall of sound will hit you when the Leafs score for the first time. Toronto's signature goal horn will blast before the fans begin the chant of "Go Leafs Go!"

6

LITTLE CAESARS ARENA

No story about hockey in Detroit can begin without talking about the octopus. Detroit is nowhere near an ocean. And the name of the NHL team is the Red Wings. The team's logo features a flying tire. But before playoff games in Detroit, fans throw octopuses onto the ice. The tradition began on April 15, 1952. The Red Wings were about to wrap up the Stanley Cup. Back then they played at Olympia Stadium. Two brothers, Pete and Jerry Cusimano, owned a fish market. When the Red Wings finished off a sweep of Montreal to win the Cup, the Cusimanos threw an octopus onto the ice.

They chose an octopus because each leg represented one of the eight playoff wins needed to capture the Cup back in those days. The number of playoff wins to raise the Cup now stands at 16. But the octopus remains important to the Red Wings, even after they moved from Olympia Stadium to Joe Louis Arena to the

LITTLE CAESARS ARENA

Detroit, Michigan

Date Opened: September 12, 2017
Capacity: 19,515
Home Team: Detroit Red Wings

brand new Little Caesars Arena. Detroit has won 11 Cups in all, seven of them since the octopus made its first appearance.

The Red Wings made Joe Louis Arena rock for decades before moving to Little Caesars Arena in 2017. The designers of the team's new home spared no expense in providing an exciting experience.

 More than a thousand lights color the ceiling of Little Caesars Arena in anticipation for Red Wings games.

The ceiling at Little Caesars Arena is unlike any other in the NHL. It has nearly 1,700 lights that can change color to add to the frenzy whenever the Red Wings score a goal. The seats on both the upper and lower levels are placed to get the fans as close to the action as possible. The lower bowl outnumbers Joe Louis Arena by 3,000 seats. The upper bowl also hangs over the lower seats to bring every fan closer to the ice than at any other NHL arena.

And just in case anyone misses a moment, replays are on the world's largest center-hung scoreboard. The scoreboard measures 28 by 43 feet (9 by 13 m).

FUN FACT

The new arena honors the Detroit arenas that came before. The original sign of Olympia Stadium hangs outside the concourse near a mural of former Red Wing great Gordie Howe.

For fans not afraid of heights, the Gondola seats deserve a try too. The seats are high up in the arena and directly above the ice. The team says it wants those seats to be the hockey version of the seats above "The Green Monster," the large wall in left field at baseball's Fenway Park in Boston.

7 XCEL ENERGY CENTER

Minnesota has long been crazy about its hockey. It doesn't matter if it's youth hockey, high school, college, or the NHL. Every winter fans flock to rinks throughout the state to take in every shift, every line change, and every goal.

Because hockey fans there have so many options, the Minnesota North Stars had trouble drawing fans. They were formed in 1967. The North Stars played at the Metropolitan Sports Center, which was located in Bloomington, Minnesota, outside of Minneapolis.

The owners grew frustrated. They wanted a new stadium. When they couldn't reach an agreement with either Minneapolis

XCEL ENERGY CENTER

St. Paul, Minnesota

Date Opened: September 29, 2000
Capacity: 17,954
Home Team: Minnesota Wild

or St. Paul, Minnesota, on a new arena, the team was sold to a group that moved the North Stars to Dallas, Texas, in 1993.

City officials in Minneapolis and St. Paul were determined not to make the same mistake twice. They badly wanted the NHL in the Twin Cities. To make sure the NHL would come back, they built a new arena.

The result was the Xcel Energy Center. Since opening its doors to welcome an expansion team, the Minnesota Wild, in 2000, the Xcel Energy Center in St. Paul has built a reputation as one of the finest hockey venues in the world.

Minnesotans love their hockey. The proof is all around the Xcel Energy Center. Jerseys from every boys and girls high school team in the state line the upper concourse.

There's even proof on the ice. In 2017 the Wild started a program called "This Is Our Ice." The program allowed fans to bring water from the state's lakes, ponds, and local rinks to the Xcel Energy Center. The water was then put in a filter and used to help create the ice the Wild skated on during the 2017–18 season.

 When the Dallas Stars returned to face Minnesota's new team, the Wild shut out the Stars behind a great performance by goalie Manny Fernandez.

Minnesotans consider their home the State of Hockey. They even have a song to prove it. Before every Wild game, the fans launch into the "State of Hockey" anthem. The song includes

 Minnesota Wild fans celebrate a playoff goal with their state's second NHL team.

the lyrics "the game is in our blood / our blood is in the game." Take one trip to the Xcel Energy Center, and it's hard to argue.

On December 17, 2000, the Dallas Stars made their first visit to Minnesota since leaving seven years earlier. The Wild exacted a little revenge for their fans with a 6–0 rout of their former home team.

Unlike the North Stars, the Wild have proven to be a hot ticket since their arrival. The team sold out its first 409 games at its new home, and interest has only grown as the team has improved.

Minnesota filled the arena 6 percent over capacity during Wild home games in the 2017–18 season, one of the top rates in the league. As Minnesotans will remind you, they're from the State of Hockey.

8 AMERICAN AIRLINES CENTER

T exas might seem like an odd place for hockey to flourish, but the Lone Star State loves sports. Texans don't just love football, baseball, and rodeos. The Minnesota North Stars relocated there in 1993. The team dropped the word *North* from their name and gave the fans in Dallas, Texas, a crash course on the NHL. It was the perfect choice in a state whose flag features a giant white star.

Nowadays the Stars are a fixture on the sports landscape in Dallas. The proof can be found every winter at American Airlines Center, where fans gather to watch the guys in black, green, and silver chase the Stanley Cup.

The Stars were immediately successful when they arrived in Dallas. Led by star forward Mike Modano, they became a hot ticket in the late 1990s while making deep playoff runs. They reached the

AMERICAN AIRLINES CENTER

Dallas, Texas

Date Opened: July 17, 2001
Capacity: 18,532
Home Team: Dallas Stars

 Texans fill the stands of the American Airlines Center during Dallas Stars games.

pinnacle in 1999 when they beat the Buffalo Sabres in the Stanley Cup Final to give the franchise its first championship.

The team moved into the flashy American Airlines Center in 2001. The arena is a mixture of high tech and Texas charm. Visitors should begin this stop by taking a tour of the wild side. The Perot Museum of Nature and Science, which is a short walk from the arena, features everything from dinosaur exhibits to a sports museum. The Sports Hall lets visitors face off in a virtual race against a cheetah or a pro football running back and learn how athletes stay in tip-top shape.

Before the puck drops, make sure to do a lap around the concourse. Model airplanes dangle from the ceiling, a nod to American Airlines.

Visiting fans should brace themselves for the singing of "The Star-Spangled Banner." Fans shout "Stars!" at the top of their lungs during the part of the national anthem that goes, "Oh say does that star-spangled banner yet wave." If the visiting team happens to score, join in with the fans as they scream "who cares" after the goal is announced over the speakers. Fans scream "Dallas! Stars!" at the top of their lungs every time the home team lights the goal lamp.

> **FUN FACT**
> The roof of American Airlines Center has more than 1 million bricks in it!

Try to come to the game hungry. The arena has plenty of Texas-themed food to munch on. Concession stands have everything from shrimp tacos to barbeque macaroni and cheese.

MAP

1. **TD Garden.** Boston, Massachusetts
2. **Madison Square Garden.** New York City, New York
3. **PPG Paints Arena.** Pittsburgh, Pennsylvania
4. **Bell Centre.** Montreal, Quebec, Canada

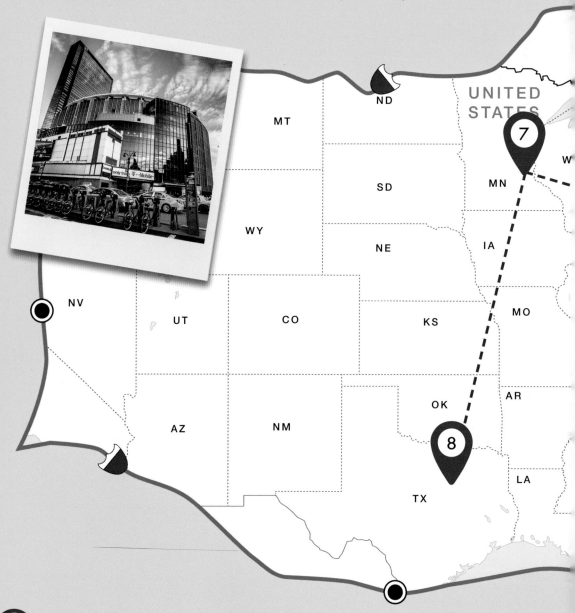

5. **Scotiabank Arena.** Toronto, Ontario, Canada
6. **Little Caesars Arena.** Detroit, Michigan
7. **Xcel Energy Center.** St. Paul, Minnesota
8. **American Airlines Center.** Dallas, Texas

Glossary

All-Star Game

An exhibition game held in the middle of every NHL season that features the top players in the league.

captain

The team leader and the only player allowed to speak to game officials regarding the rules.

center ice

A red dot in the middle of a hockey rink, where faceoffs are held at the start of each period and after every goal.

expansion

The addition of new teams to increase the size of a league.

overtime

An extra period of play when the score is tied after regulation.

relocate

To move a franchise from one city to another.

rout

To defeat decisively or disastrously.

Stanley Cup

The trophy given to the team that wins the NHL playoffs each season.

More Information

BOOKS

Graves, Will. *The Best Hockey Players of All Time*. Minneapolis, MN: Abdo Publishing, 2015.

Kortemeier, Todd. *Total Hockey*. Minneapolis, MN: Abdo Publishing, 2017.

Martin, Brett S. *STEM in Hockey*. Minneapolis, MN: Abdo Publishing, 2018.

Online Resources

Booklinks
NONFICTION NETWORK
FREE! ONLINE NONFICTION RESOURCES

To learn more about NHL arenas, visit **abdobooklinks.com**. These links are routinely monitored and updated to provide the most current information available.

Index

About the Author

Will Graves grew up in the Washington, DC, suburbs rooting every year for the Washington Capitals to win the Stanley Cup. Graves has spent more than two decades as a sportswriter. He works for the Associated Press in Pittsburgh, Pennsylvania, where he covers the NFL, the NHL, and Major League Baseball as well as the Olympics.